The Rialto Prom

A Play

Angela Wye

A Samuel French Acting Edition

SAMUEL FRENCH

FOUNDED 1830

SAMUELFRENCH-LONDON.CO.UK
SAMUELFRENCH.COM

THE RIALTO PROM

First performed as an Inter-Action production at the Almost Free Theatre, London, on the 21st October 1974, with the following cast of characters:

Avril	Ann Mitchell
Enid	Margie Campi
Doreen	Jacquie Cook
Sandra	Elizabeth Estensen
Lynda	Linda Beckett

The play directed by Sue Todd
Settings by Norman Coates

The action takes place outside and in the cloakroom of the Rialto Ballroom, Liverpool

Time – the present

AUTHOR'S NOTE

The play is set in Liverpool. It is very important and very necessary that all the characters speak with either a Lancashire or Liverpudlian accent. It would be inappropriate to write a description of each character as this, I believe, can only serve to block creative imagination. Vision should spring from the text aided by the casual emphasis of a stage direction.

However, I feel that the age range of the characters should be established, and would favour the following guidelines:

Avril, thirty or the wrong side of it.

Enid, middle twenties to thirty.

Doreen, middle to late twenties.

Sandra, middle twenties.

Lynda, early to middle twenties.

THE RIALTO PROM

SCENE 1

Outside the Rialto Ballroom, Liverpool

When the Curtain *rises, Avril is showing signs of impatience, strolling up and down, as the wait for her friends lengthens unbearably. After a few moments there is a shout off from Enid as she approaches*

Enid (*off*) AV-AS—WHOEE—I'm here . . .

Avril goes and looks in the direction of the voice

Enid enters bouncily

Enid Bet you thought I'd be late?
Avril (*curtly*) You are!
Enid (*taken aback*) Oh, just a shade.
Avril Yes, late. And with a bloody trumpet voluntary. D'you need to let everyone know where we're going?
Enid Thought that were obvious, anyway. T'others inside?

Avril looks exasperated

Oh, I get it; they're not here yet.
Avril Oh we are observant, Enid.
Enid Oh dear, pissed off with waiting, are we? Well, there's one thing, hanging about you'll have burnt up a few calories.
Avril (*sarcastically*) Yes, the heat loss 'as been tremendous. I'm bloody froze. Been standing here for nigh on twenty minutes.
Enid Whose fault is that? You could have walked up and down.
Avril What? And be taken for a bloody pick-up? Not likely!

Enid turns her attention to adjusting her clothes

Obsessed with diet talk, that's you.
Enid I'm not. I'm not even on one yet. Just thinking about starting tomorrow.

Avril (*sarcastically*) Oh yes, you're always thinking. (*Pause*) Did Doreen say she wasn't coming, like?

Enid Not a word. Late home, I should think.

Avril Well, didn't I rush. Didn't I break me neck to get here. Wasn't I in such a rush I had to paint me nails on the bus.

Enid You didn't?

Avril And why not? I were upstairs.

Enid (*elbowing Avril and pointing off*) Hey, is that them just got off that bus?

Avril peers in the direction Enid is pointing

Avril Well, unless they're walking backwards they would appear to be going in the opposite direction.

Enid Could be a trick. (*She moves away*) What's the talent like, have you noticed?

Avril Only what to avoid.

Enid Worth the entrance money?

Avril Well, we've always managed to break even.

Enid Still, it's early yet. The night is young, as they say. I was hoping that—well, you know, I might see . . .

Avril A week is a long time.

Enid I know, but I kept him in me thoughts 'till Thursday.

Avril You always had a vivid imagination.

Enid No, honest, it's a good sign if you can still think of somebody five days after you've met them.

Avril It's curtains, Enid, I told you that. As soon as I saw him I told you the type.

Enid You did, but you may be wrong.

Avril Anyways on, we're here to enjoy ourselves, help other people enjoy themselves, and altogether have a bloody good time. (*She holds her thumbs up*) Clickety-click.

Enid joins in simultaneously clicking fingers and swinging her leg with Avril in the "fun sign" routine

Enid (*thumbs up*) Clickety-click. 'Ey, Avril, would you be very cross if I told you Sonia wasn't coming?

Avril Not coming? For why?

Enid She's got sick.

Avril On a Saturday? When we've been so good to her, done so much, tried to help . . .

Enid Aye, I know, but her mother has too.

Avril What? What the 'ell are yer talking about?

Enid Proper poorly is Sonia, proper poorly. Her mother said so. She said she won't be coming no more, Miss Enid, no more.

Avril No more? Why? She was looking forward to it. She told me herself. She even smiled.

Enid Perhaps it were easier.

Avril Are you telling me she was having me on? I see. Taking me for a bloody ride. That's gratitude. How's that for a bleeding favour.

Enid Don't take on about it. It isn't the first time and it won't be the last. (*After a slight pause, elbowing Avril*) 'Ere, d'you see that bloke that went in? The neat one? He came to our house today. Gave me some Bible cards.

Avril Bible cards?

Enid Said he were a Catholic.

Avril Oh Jesus!

Enid That's right, he mentioned him. He was real interesting, you know. Asked me down to the club, down St Edmund's.

Avril You're not going, are you? They're not all like him, you know. He's what you call a loss leader. Like you have in the supermarkets to entice you in. You know what, it's even rumoured they give you Green Shield stamps on your first visit. Always recruiting, are the Catholics. They'd think of anything.

Enid Orange Lodge talk is that. I can go if I want to. Fancy him coming here, then.

Avril Fancy; before you know it the last waltz'll be a hymn.

Enid D'you think he's going to try and convert people?

Avril On a Saturday? He'll be lucky.

Enid Give out leaflets and that.

Avril Well, I didn't notice him carrying any—unless, of course, he had them in his 'andbag.

They both burst out laughing

(*Becoming serious*) Is Sandra bringing a friend, then, if Sonia's not coming?

Enid They won't let you down, you know. Doreen's a good scout.

Avril Just asking.

Enid As a matter of fact, I knows who it is.
Avril You're keeping a lot of things to yourself, it seems to me.
Enid Tell me, have you eaten?
Avril Why?
Enid I never chance telling you anything on an empty stomach.
Avril I had a cheese roll, you know—and an apricot tart. And yours, put on the bloody table in front of you, I suppose? What it is to have a mother who dotes on you at your age.
Enid I am the youngest.
Avril The baby, eh? How touching, how very touching. (*She snaps*) You are watching for the buses, aren't you?
Enid I'm watching. (*Pause*) Seen your mother lately?
Avril She comes and goes. The old man's got a housekeeper now.
Enid That's posh.
Avril The question is, is she on to a good thing or is he? Funny 'ow men change.
Enid Why don't you get out—get a place of your own?
Avril Why should I be driven out? Anyways on, we only meet on the stairs. Me brother's there as well, you know. He's just bought a new bed—a double. Kept falling out of the single. He got used to it, but his birds didn't. It played hell on our nerves, they would keep screaming. For weeks we had no proper sleep.

Enid roars with laughter

Enid Oh, I do think that's funny.
Avril Oh ay, you would. The trouble now is, the bed only fits in the room one way—under the leak.
Enid (*laughing*) What d'you do, pray for rain or give them umbrellas?

Avril does not laugh

Laugh, Avril. Laugh and the world might too.
Avril (*snapping*) 'Ere, you run your life, and I'll run mine.
Enid Just a friendly remark, I'm sure.
Avril (*sighing*) It don't half take something out of you, all this waiting. And you know what you're like in the cloakroom. It takes you ages to doll up and 'flate yer boobs.
Enid (*countering*) Realign the straps.

Avril Don't know why you don't just slip a knot in them and be done.

Enid Can I help it if I have to give extra care to what I've got?

Avril Reckon it were all that swimming. Never did a thing for me. If they worry you, you know, you can have an operation. They take a piece out like a big wedge of cake and sew you back together again. Good as new. And never again will you tip over on a slope.

Enid I'm not neurotic about them, but it sounds as though you are. (*Uppishly*) Just make the best use of what I've got.

Avril Yes, and I make the best use of what I haven't. I've told you before, you only have to make sure you get a bum fancier, that's the trick.

They both appear to be watching a figure walking past on the opposite side of the road

Could have sworn that was Sandra.

Enid She never wears green. The height's wrong.

Avril You're right, not on a Saturday. Dead image, could have sworn. Feet un all. 'Ey up, if looks could kill.

Enid And a gesture to go with them. (*She does just that*)

Avril Don't stare, Enid. Manners!

Enid *Don't* tell me.

Avril (*sounding Enid out*) I say, Enid, that Sonia, she didn't do anything—I mean, didn't do anything daft, like? She didn't try anything daft?

Enid I wasn't going to tell you?

Avril Well, I'm asking, aren't I? I'm asking.

Enid is pensive

Of course, it were probably bluff. She wouldn't have the guts. Nobody'd be taken in.

Enid She could have done better, I must say. The Mersey's not the best way.

Avril The Mersey?

Enid Tried to drown herself.

Avril In the Mersey? Even I can think of better ways.

Enid She couldn't. Lay down and waited for the tide to come in. It didn't. Or rather, she was spotted from the prom. The Panda boys on patrol.

Avril There you are, it were fate. She wasn't meant to die.

Enid There'd be thousands say she was.
Avril And I quite liked her, you know. Quite liked her.

A short, awkward pause

Enid (*nudging Avril*) 'Ey, look 'o's on the horizon all of a
    sudden. Blowed if it's not our . . .
Avril Doreen—at last!

*Doreen enters, breathless and walking with difficulty in tight
shoes, and chewing gum*

Doreen Oh dear, I'm fagged out. (*Blowing*) I wish I'd worn
    roller skates. Who'd have thought I could never rush in these
    shoes. Still, have I beaten the others?

Avril and Enid nod

    They're not far behind, then.
Avril The least said, don't you think, Enid?
Enid Oh, I do, Avril. The least said.
Doreen Well, thanks for the warm, friendly greeting. Better get
    inside, then. Like I say, they're on their way.
Avril Let's go. Catch us up, they'll have to. Clickety-click.
Enid ⎱Clickety-click. ⎰ *Speaking*
Doreen ⎰   ⎱ *together*

They all make for the entrance arm in arm

Avril Now let me see, what is it I ask for? One and two halves?

They all peal with laughter as the Lights fade

SCENE 2

A cubicle-like corner of the ladies' cloakroom

*The surroundings bear the stamp of mass-produced "chain-group"
elegance in the design. Both walls are covered by mirrors with
mounted lights. At waist level a handbag shelf runs under the
mirrors. There are four stools in the area. It is evident that the
greater part of the cloakroom is off stage, along with the entrance*

Doreen, Avril and Enid enter, and synchronize the placing of their handbags on the shelf, taking their money from their pockets and removing their coats

Doreen (*still chewing gum*) Who's taking the coats, then, to old fart-face out there?

The coats are passed to Doreen without a word, by the other two. Avril faces the mirror and puts the finishing touches to her appearance. Enid titivates

Can't think why you go to so much trouble when it's half dark out there.

Avril You'd be surprised what shows up when a bloke uses a lighter.

Enid Or strikes a match. Always aim to please. Isn't that right, Avril?

Avril (*condescendingly*) That's right, Enid, it's a start.

Doreen gathers the coats together in her arms to take them out, collecting money from Avril and Enid on the way

Enid She's on to a good thing, is old fart-face. She'll think she's bloody cloakroom attendant of the year.

Doreen I'd sooner give her money than have me coat sold.

Doreen exits with the coats and money

Enid She frightens me to death. The way she hovers at the toilet door, cloth in hand, daring me—just daring me to wet the seat. Enough to give you retention for weeks.

Some titivating goes on. Avril finishes at the mirror and calls

Avril Zip . . . !

Enid obeys the call and undoes the back of Avril's dress just far enough for Avril to plunge her hand down and adjust her bra straps. Enid returns to her mirror, trying to decide how she should wear her blouse, in or out of her skirt

Doreen returns

Having achieved her adjustment, Avril calls out again

Zip . . . !

This time Doreen steps forward to do the zip up. Avril turns her attention to Enid

Time's getting on, Enid. Have you done?
Enid I can't decide whether this blouse looks better in or out.
Avril Neither.

Doreen laughs quietly

Enid It's new, you know.
Avril What's that got to do with it?
Enid Thought I'd mention it.
Doreen Out of the catalogue, is it?
Enid What if it is?
Doreen Before you buy things, you should try them on.
Enid That's no answer. Things always look different after you've bought them. Anyway, it looked all right in the book. It was all they had in blue. I wanted blue. It's this mirror, it's not good in a bad light.
Doreen Mirrors don't lie.
Avril Only bloody men.
Enid (*turning round to Doreen*) How is it then that in the spare room at home, I looked quite different?
Doreen Probably had your eyes closed and the door shut.
Enid (*snapping*) You are awful. You don't half give a girl confidence, you two.
Avril Appreciated at last, are we?
Enid You'll make me feel so bad soon I won't dare to go in there unless I'm stark naked.
Avril There you are, you see, Doreen, she has got good dress sense after all.

Enid sighs, defeated by the sparring

Doreen (*still sparring*) What I can't get over is the sudden passion for blue. Or has somebody else?
Enid Mind yours.
Avril I've tried to tell her. They never come two wecks on the trot.
Doreen It's not happened yet. (*She moves close to Avril*)
Enid (*with a burst of antagonism*) Well, one day you're going to

be wrong. Somebody's going to turn up twice. Somebody's going to. Somebody's bloody going to.

There is an awkward pause. Doreen and Avril flash quick looks at each other, and Doreen speaks to ease the situation

Doreen I should wear your blouse tucked in, love. Show off your waist. (*Still close to Avril, she chews her gum*)
Avril (*irritably*) For God's sake, Doreen, stop chewing that bloody gum in my ear. I can't think for the noise.
Doreen All right. (*Taking the gum out of her mouth*) It's worn out, anyway. (*She sticks the gum on the underside of the handbag shelf*)
Enid (*seizing the chance to get her own back*) They only chew gum at football matches, never dances.
Avril She's right. It's the only thing that can make me watch football on the telly.
Doreen What? Chewing gum?
Avril Yes, I'm waiting—all the time I'm waiting for some footballer to choke. Ever since that doctor said a piece of chewing gum lodged in the windpipe could kill, I've sat there fascinated.
Doreen They call that morbid curiosity.
Avril Which reminds me, Enid, if you want to be the honey-pot of the evening, how about taking your bra off and trying that for appeal?
Enid Not likely, last time I did that I got a cold.
Avril You can still wear a vest.
Doreen (*laughing*) At least if you took your bra off to provide a little titillation you might bust the competition.

They all laugh

Sandra, carrying a case and a paper carrier-bag enters with Lynda. Lynda is nervously hanging back, timid and obviously out of place

Sandra Hello, hello, hello. What's this, then—mirth and merriment? Did I hear somebody talking about competition, 'cause it's here. We've arrived—us . . .

They all stare at Lynda. Sandra moves across to bring her forward.

Lynda, I want you to meet Avril—Doreen—Enid. Avril—
Doreen—Enid—Lynda . . .

Lynda manages a nervous grin

Doreen We have met. Charmed, I'm sure.

*Lynda brings forward a box of chocolates she has been nervously
clutching*

Lynda I've brought some chocolates.
Avril Oh, that is nice, Lynda. But it's not quite like a theatre
outing, is dancing.
Lynda (*missing the point*) Chocolates, dairy and plain.
Avril (*taking the box as the easiest way out*) Yes, thank you,
Lynda. We'll put them here for later. (*She puts them on the
shelf*)
Doreen I'll take your coats to fart-face. She's had her eyes on
yours, Sandra, for a long time.

Sandra playfully threatens Doreen by raising an arm

Sandra Ger-away! (*She gives Doreen her coat*)

Lynda awkwardly takes off her coat and gives it to Doreen

Doreen exits with the coats

Enid (*giving Lynda a stool*) Sit down, Lynda.
Lynda (*nervously*) I've never been—to a dance—before. Only
evening classes. (*She sits on a stool at one end*)
Avril One and the same, aren't they, Sandra? One and the
same.
Sandra Lynda's been doing pottery classes for ages now. You
should see her house. Full of ashtrays and plant pots and
things. Her mother thought she should have a change—to
help her creativity.
Lynda Last week I finished a dog bowl.
Sandra That's right—her twenty-fifth.
Lynda (*with pride*) Yes.
Enid (*to Sandra*) And now you're going to tell us they haven't
got a dog.
Lynda (*overhearing*) No, but we're going to get one.

They all try not to laugh

Doreen enters and sits on a stool

Doreen Has no-one opened the chocolates, then? Don't all rush and pass me one. (*She reaches for the box and gets stuck in*)
Enid Sandra, aren't we forgetting something? (*Nodding towards Lynda*) Has she had her bath?
Avril Shaved her legs?
Doreen Under her arms?
Avril Cut her toenails?
Enid Cleaned her teeth?
Sandra Washed her hair?
Doreen (*stuffing chocolates into her mouth*) Had her bowels open?

They all dart a look at Doreen

Sandra The list, she had the list. That's why we're a bit late.
Lynda Oh yes, I had the list.
Doreen (*aside to Avril*) You'll be asking her next if she's got name tapes on her knickers. Give the girl a chance, Avril, do you want her to be bloody gift-wrapped?
Avril Just oven-ready, you twat—oven-ready.
Enid (*to Lynda*) Well, we are a bit stuck here for facilities, Lynda, you understand.
Lynda Sandra told me that.
Avril You did put your clean underwear on, now didn't you, Lynda? You know the rules—parties and doctors.
Lynda Oh yes, Sandra told me that.
Doreen Have a chocolate, Lynda, one of yours. (*She holds out the box*)
Sandra (*pushing the box away*) She's got a spot.
Enid (*to Avril*) She's got a spot.
Avril (*to Doreen*) She's got a spot.
Sandra Her best side, too.

Avril takes Lynda to a stool in the middle of the group and sits her on it

Avril (*studying her*) Now, sit there a minute, love.

The others surround Lynda

Now turn to the right—and the other way. Mmm—ought to squeeze it.

Sandra It looks ripe.
Enid It won't notice if she sits the other way on. Out there.
Avril Lynda, love, I think we ought to do a little cosmetic surgery. Nothing painful, you understand. (*Holding out her hand*) Tissue . . .

Doreen places a tissue in Avril's hand. Avril advances on Lynda to squeeze the spot. Sandra stands behind Lynda, holding her head still. Lynda moans with discomfort

Sandra That's it. All done. A bit of make-up'll do the trick.
Lynda (*fingering the spot*) It's flatter.
Doreen Have a chocolate?
Sandra Keep the tissue on it, stop it running.
Doreen A chocolate for being good.
Lynda Could I have a nutty one?
Doreen Sorry, love, those have gone. Turkish Delight or Orange Contessa?

Lynda is just about to put her hand in the box when Avril pushes Doreen's arm away

Avril We've got work to do.

However, they all manage to take a chocolate before the box goes back on the shelf

Lynda Oh—oh—I think I feel funny.
Sandra Lynda, you're not coming over queer, are you?
Avril Put her head down.
Doreen She's not going to be sick, is she?
Avril Smelling salts.
Enid That's the last thing we've got.
Doreen Eau-de-Cologne. (*She rummages in her handbag and produces a small bottle*) A little bottle, how about that?
Sandra Try it. Try it.

Doreen sniffs at the bottle

Enid (*snatching the bottle away*) On Lynda, you fool.

Enid holds the bottle under Lynda's nose, getting a slight reaction

There, that's better. Breathe deeply, now. In and out. In and out.

Sandra That's right, in and out, deep breaths.
Doreen Just add a chorus of "bear downs" and it'll sound like a flaming labour ward.

Enid and Avril glare at Doreen

Lynda (*sniffing and breathing deeply*) Lovely—lovely—what is it? Oil of cloves or something?

Taken aback by her ignorance, they all shoot looks at one another

Avril Or something.
Sandra There now, your colour's coming back. You're coming back to life.
Lynda (*stuttering*) I'm—ever so sorry—I don't know what it was that came over me. I've never done that before. Maybe I shouldn't have come.
Enid Don't say that.
Doreen Well, not yet, anyway.

Avril shoots Doreen a look

Lynda (*fingering her spot*) I did lose some blood—perhaps it was that. I never could stand the sight of it.
Avril Well, that's as maybe, Lynda. Let's forget all about it. (*Turning to the others*) What d'you say, girls? (*She puts her thumbs up*) Clickety-click.

They all break into the fun sign routine, moving to Lynda

Doreen
Enid   } Clickety-click. { *Speaking together*
Sandra

Avril That's our fun sign, Lynda. You'll have to learn to do that if you're coming with us.
Lynda I'd like to.
Avril That's the spirit, participation.

They all bubble with laughter, with Lynda not quite on the ball

Lynda Me mother plays Bingo.
Sandra Does she win?
Lynda She won a biro once—it didn't work very well.
Enid Then there's luck in your family!
Lynda Me mum's had better with the horses.
Sandra We could do with a few tips.

Lynda Horses with seven letters. She always chooses them.
Enid And four legs and all?
Avril Let's have less chat. There's no time for a lot of pissing about. Lynda doesn't want to stop here all night discussing form. She wants action. The bag, Sandra, the bag.

Sandra brings over the carrier bag and opens it. They all gather round Lynda

Now, Lynda, that's a very nice dress you're wearing. Home sewn, is it? Well, we thought—we thought this evening we'd help you to be a real smash. On your first visit . . .
Enid Really make an entrance . . .
Doreen An unforgettable vision . . .
Sandra For that certain somebody.
Avril That's right. We've got a little something. Something for Saturdays. We've thought about it a lot.
Doreen A great deal.
Sandra We really care.
Avril Here, then. Specially for you. For beauty—black.

With a flourish Enid sweeps the gown from the bag

Enid Real sexy, is that.
Doreen Black for beautiful Saturdays.
Avril We'll swop it for what you've got on. One pound now and four pounds fifty later.
Sandra Spread over, like.
Avril To cover our expenses, you understand.

There is a slight pause

Doreen You like it, Lynda, don't you?
Lynda Er . . . (*She swallows hard*) I've never worn black.
Avril That's why we're giving you the chance. Not everyone gets the opportunity to wear an—(*she peers at the label in the neck of the dress*) a Samantha Young.

Enid, Avril and Sandra feign a breathtaking gasp at the same time. Doreen speaks in a Hollywood style

Doreen A Samantha Young—oh . . . !
Lynda Would it fit me? I'm not sure. I'm not sure I'd look right in black.

Avril Don't worry your head about things like that. Leave the big decisions to us, love.

Lynda But . . .

Avril We're going to do our very best for you. No question of that. We've given it a lot of thought.

Lynda But . . .

Doreen Don't worry. Money on account, cheques, luncheon vouchers—all the same to us.

Lynda Me mam said, carry enough for a taxi home, that's all.

Avril Oh now, didn't Sandra tell you we have a little rule?

Enid and Avril start removing Lynda's dress, somewhat to her surprise also to be taken off in the preparation are Lynda's locket and watch

First one to get a lift home gets a lift for all of us. It works very well. That way no-one loses out.

Sandra fetches the case with the make-up and starts to check the contents. Doreen takes the wigs out and sits combing them

Enid I have known it to be otherwise.

Avril Oh, and your grouse?

Enid Last time it was my lift, and I was the one that got dropped off first.

Avril And is it our fault that you proved to be a rotten traveller?

Sandra It was a test of stamina. Eight circuits of the Speke roundabout . . .

Doreen And two U-turns on the Warrington M'way.

Enid Yes, but it were your nerves he was trying to break, not mine. He wanted to be rid of you.

Avril We'd never have guessed. Anyway, he had his chance, the pick of the pieces. (*Pause*) I wonder if that were one of the things to stop Sonia coming this week.

Sandra I bet it didn't help.

By this time Lynda is standing awkwardly in her very plain under-wear

Avril 'Ey up, we're waffling now, when Lynda's waiting here to put her dress on. Oh, and Lynda, one thing. No looking in the mirror. No cheating. Not 'til we've got you up proper. Not 'til we've finished you, like. Promise us that. Here, Enid, it's all yours,

Lynda is pushed forward and Enid puts on the black halter-neck dress. Sandra gets the shoes for Lynda from the case

(*To Sandra*) Y've changed your job again?

Sandra What of it?

Avril What does that make it? Eight jobs in ten weeks?

Enid She prefers you to say ten weeks in eight jobs. It creates an aural illusion.

Sandra So, I'm a career girl. You should know that.

Doreen And the new job, where is it?

Sandra Why should I tell you? Anyway, each time I've moved I've got better money.

Avril And better things.

Sandra (*bringing the shoes*) Will we get the shoes on?

Avril See to it that we do.

Doreen and Enid put the shoes on Lynda

Sandra I'd be daft not to take advantage of the special arrangements.

Doreen M'mm that you should be so lucky. When I think of the perks in my job. Old Saunders gives me a calendar at Christmas, violet creams at Easter, a wish-you-were-here holiday card and a packet of mint tea. If only he could think of something different. Just once.

Avril A man? A bloody man? (*Pause*) If you had ambition you wouldn't stick it.

Doreen I've told you before. It's handy for travelling.

Lynda's bra straps can be seen, now that she has the dress on

Avril The bra, Enid, the bra.

Enid takes Lynda's bra off, pulling it through the halter-neck of the dress, before Lynda realizes what is happening

All right, Lynda? You're looking great. You're becoming something—a dream. Do you know that? A dream coming true.

Automatically Lynda moves to look in the mirror, but is stopped by the group blocking her path

Ah, not yet, not 'till we've finished. Remember, remember

that. (*Pause*) Now love, your hair. Your crowning glory. We've got to do something with that. I can see it's very fine.

Sandra produces a large pair of scissors, and makes a move to cut Lynda's hair. Lynda shrinks. Avril dismisses the scissors

Not tonight, Sandra. I'm not in the mood. (*To Doreen, who is still attending to the wigs*) Something more instant, Doreen?

Doreen holds up a blonde and an auburn wig

(*To Lynda*) Now Lynda, do you have a fancy?
Lynda Well, I . . .
Avril That's what I thought—the blonde.

Doreen skilfully places the blonde wig on Lynda in view of the audience. The other girls move to view. Lynda's natural reaction is to get up to the mirror. Sandra restrains her

Sandra Not yet, Lynda. After all, when we're born we don't get a look-see. We don't know what we're going to look like then.
Avril (*commenting on the wig*) Well, I can't say I'm gone on that one much.

Avril and Doreen synchronize a move to view Lynda from the front

M'mm. Close your eyes a minute, love, so we can see what it would look like if you were lying down.
Enid It's not quite right, is it. The auburn, you'll have to try that.

Doreen and Avril briskly snatch the wig off Lynda and throw it on the shelf. Doreen brings forward the auburn wig and Lynda is smartly placed on a stool with her back to the audience. Doreen efficiently tries the wig on—the effects from now on being unseen by the audience

Avril Yes, I think that's the one. That's it.

The others nod their approval

A dream, Lynda, you look just that. Coming true, a dream. We've only the make-up, now. Just a touch to make your fascination devastatingly certain.

Enid brings forward the box of make-up equipment, handing a chart to Sandra for consultation

Sandra (*to Enid, reading from the chart*) Foundation—"Sunlit Glow" or "Tango Pink".

Enid hands the bottle/stick to Avril, who gets to work

Eyelashes—"Sweeping Peepers".

Doreen—the efficient hair expert—places the lashes on Lynda's eyes

Eye shadow and lipstick—"Sudden Arrangement" and—(*she runs her finger along the chart*)—and lipstick "Claret Sorbet".

Avril applies the eye shadow and then the lipstick and other finishing touches. She reflects on her artistic achievement and is reminded of the presence of the others only when Enid clicks her bag shut

Avril Oh God, you lot still here. There's not the time to be stood standing there and bloody staring. Not when there's things to be done. (*She waves the others away*) Things to be done—places, everyone—places . . .

The Lights fade

SCENE 3

The same. Some minutes later

When the Lights come up Avril and Lynda are discovered sitting on stools. Avril is closely viewing Lynda. After a moment she sighs with satisfaction. Already the make-up makes Lynda look bizarre

Avril Fantastic, Lynda. (*Gesturing to Lynda to stand*) Stand up a moment, love. Stand up.

Lynda stands

Very effective. Good. You'll hook a few tonight. There's no mistake about that. Might even cause a fight.

Lynda makes a move as if to look in the mirror. Avril stops her

Lynda (*nervously*) I was thinking.

Avril Yes, you have been quiet.

Lynda (*worried*) I—I can't dance.

Avril Oh, that won't matter, there won't be much time for that. (*As an afterthought*) Not when it's crowded, like.

Lynda I don't know anybody.

Avril We're all equal there.

Lynda Yes, but—you have been before.

Avril It's nerves you've got. You'll be fine when you get out there with a purpose. You'll be the main attraction. Get that straight.

Lynda But I'm not cut out for it. I thought it'd be different. I thought I'd feel different.

Avril Well you have been in a trance, then. This is an occasion you have to rise to. Most girls'd be glad of the chance. Any man in that room . . .

Lynda I never thought . . .

Avril puts Lynda in a sex-symbol pose, raising one of her legs on a stool, placing her hand on her hip, moving her head back to one side

Avril Like I said, you haven't been in there yet. Reserve your judgement for the happy occasion. Dreams can come true. We know how the system works, finding out for yourself— that's called experience, and that's worth having. Think big. There's ways of dancing with men that they've never heard of.

Doreen enters with three glasses of gin-and-tonic on a tray

Doreen Here we are, then. A little something for the launching. No need to turn pale, Lynda. You won't have to glide down a slipway or anything. (*She puts the tray on the shelf and hands round the drinks. To Lynda*) Just one thing, love. When you've drunk this, keep away from a naked light. (*She laughs*)

Avril laughs. Doreen turns her attention to the other side of the cloakroom and fart-face off stage

(*Raising her glass*) Love and kisses, fart-face. Cheers. (*To Lynda*) Gin-and-tonic, double. Sip it while it's hot. (*She laughs*)

Avril laughs

Lynda (*drinking her gin rather quickly*) I've never had gin before. At Christmas me mother buys port and sherry. We have whisky, but only for accidents. She keeps it in the cupboard with the elastoplast and the Enos.

Doreen What a tragedy. A girl's best friend is gin.

Avril It had its day, shall we say. Don't drink it so quick, Lynda, or it'll miss your head and go straight to your feet . . .

Doreen Curl up your toes and turn your pubic hair green. (*She laughs*)

Avril Must your mouth open when you want to speak in that manner. I'd rather you tried breathing another way and made yourself useful. Lynda needs a little finishing off—a little attention to her adornment. Some jewellery from the box.

Doreen brings out of the case a large box and looks inside it, picking out jewellery

Doreen Now, what should we have? The Krupp diamond? Betty Hutton's pearls or Regina's emeralds? It's not an easy decision. Which d'you fancy?

Lynda has no chance to choose because Avril soon intervenes

Avril Give me the box. Are you people going to take all night? (*She takes the box*) Have I got to do everything? (*She takes out a brooch*) The gold amethyst. That's the one. On black it always looks good. (*She gives it to Doreen*) Put it on.

Doreen puts in on Lynda. Avril dips into the box again

Bracelets—rings a little jingle-jangle. Your hand—hold it out, love.

Lynda holds out her right hand

T'other one. Bracelets only on the left, no rings. Not yet, anyway. If it's a busy evening ahead you can make your ring finger awful sore. (*She finishes decorating Lynda with rings and bracelets and once more steps back for a long-distance view*)

Although it is necessary for Lynda to look embarrassingly awful, the image must not be too extreme

There now, let me see. Another look. Victory for art and design, wouldn't you say, Doreen?

Doreen moves to Avril's vantage point

Doreen Quite definitely. The conquest of nature. Better at it than
  our Creator.
Avril Well, he were a man! They make mistakes like everybody
  else. You're a dream come true, Lynda. The perfect woman
  created by woman with man in mind.
Doreen Follow that—the advertiser's nightmare.

*Once more Lynda attempts to look in the mirror, and again her
attention is diverted*

Avril (*producing a packet of cigarettes*) A cigarette, love? Have a
  cig. (*Suddenly withdrawing the packet*) On second thoughts,
  don't. It's a filthy habit. (*She lights up for herself. To Doreen*)
  You gave her a double gin?
Doreen Should have been a treble.

A slight pause. Avril blows smoke into Lynda's face

Avril Now, Lynda love, we must think of other things. A body
  must have a mind. You've never been to a dance before, have
  you?
Doreen Another mistake.
Lynda I said.
Avril You did. I think we should talk about it. Before you go—
  out there . . .
Doreen On the floor. It being your first time, like. It helps to
  know—
Avril —what it's like—
Doreen —out there.
Avril Questions—perhaps you've questions?
Lynda Well, I . . .
Avril Didn't think you would, not yet.
Doreen Later, perhaps, when you know—
Avril —what it's like—out there . . .
Doreen To be a pilgrim.
Sandra (*off, slightly inebriated, talking to fart-face*) Down the
  hatch to turn the latch. Cheers—cheers . . .

*Giggling at fart-face, Sandra enters, glass in hand, and is on top
of the others before realizing it*

Doreen We've been waiting for you.
Sandra I'm a busy person—busy life. (*At Lynda*) Who's this? Aren't you going to introduce me? At once!

Avril nods at Doreen

Doreen Sandra, meet Lyn—er—Brenda.
Lynda (*with a grin*) Er—Lynda—Lynda Barnsley ...
Avril No, *Brenda*.
Sandra (*putting out her hand*) Charmed, delighted—pleased to meet you ... (*She sniggers*)
Lynda (*jumping up*) But it's me—it's me ...

Sandra just grins

Avril (*to Lynda*) Sit down, love, do.

Lynda sits

There's no need to stand on ceremony, not with us. No need at all, *Brenda*.
Lynda (*swallowing hard*) But ...
Avril But nothing. It's no good living in the past. Not on a Saturday. You'd better meet her. Take a look-see—
Doreen —before you go out there.
Lynda But ...
Sandra Remember, we don't see ourselves as others see us—not never—
Doreen —on a Saturday.
Avril Spoil yourself. Indulge. Take a dekko. Go on, before you go—out there.

They all gaze at Lynda, almost daring her to look in the mirror

Lynda (*clenching her hands*) I can't. I'd rather not. I don't want to.

A slight pause

Doreen Don't?
Avril For why?
Lynda I—I don't feel right.
Sandra After all this, you don't feel right?
Lynda No, all of a sudden, I don't.
Doreen Not at all. You haven't felt it coming on.
Lynda No, I ...

Avril And beautiful people, do they have to feel it, I'm asking?
Lynda Ay—I think they do.
Doreen You can tell, can you? How?
Lynda By the way they walk.
Sandra Oh my God.
Lynda Enid would know what I meant—if she were here.
Avril She would, would she? We must think on this. And where
is Enid when she's wanted?

Sandra and Doreen look at each other

Sandra Oh yes, well—er—she's following . . .
Doreen That's right—following . . .
Avril So long as you keep me in the know, that's all. In the
know.
Sandra Yes—well—there's a lot to think about. You know what
Enid is, slow and deliberate, very slow. Likes to take her time.
Doreen (*creating a diversion*) Slow, slow, quick, quick, slow.
Slow, slow, quick, quick, slow. They're playing our tune . . .
Sandra (*pointing at Doreen*) She wants watching. She'll have her
tap shoes out next.

Sandra and Doreen laugh

Avril Unconscious music, they call that, going back to another
era. Always thought she was older than she said. (*To Lynda*)
Can you hear the band—out there?
Lynda Can't say I . . .
Avril Exactly, no good pretending.
Doreen Can't hear the band? Then listen. (*She picks up an ash-
tray from the handbag shelf and puts it to Lynda's ear*)
   The Mersey lapping the shores of Otterspool,
   On the sunkissed burning sand;
   Where the slops meet the shore in their sewers
   And you cover your nose with your hand.
(*She laughs*)

*Sandra jogs around to the music in her head from the hall. Doreen
catches on to the beat*

Lynda I can't hear anything.
Doreen M'mm, let's try the other ear, it may have a bigger hole.
Lynda Don't . . .

Sandra If you can't hear anything, don't worry. It only means the tide's out for another week.

Doreen Pipe down, you—that's my line.

Sandra I'm trying to make it a good evening.

Avril Well, don't try too hard.

Sandra (*cockily*) I don't have to.

Avril Oh, and what have you achieved—out there?

Sandra Interested, are you?

Doreen (*to Lynda*) Take note of this, love. You might learn something. How to be a woman.

Lynda But I haven't got a pencil.

Doreen (*touching her head*) Here, up here.

Avril Hey up, Enid's not back. She's missing all the fun.

Sandra Er—following—I said . . .

Avril Some time ago.

Sandra Ah, well, you see—she sat down—at the far end of the hall. (*To Lynda*) You should never do that—at a dance—sit down—it's difficult to get up—never sit down—unless you've something to do—eating, drinking—or the other, you know— it puts women in an inferior position—sitting down—at a dance—gets you trapped—puts you wrong for the evening—in a subordinate situation . . .

Doreen (*to Lynda*) You see, you can't ask a man to dance—

Avril —not in so many words.

Sandra But you can say *No*—

Avril —more than once, so it hurts.

Doreen You've nothing to lose—

Avril —but they have.

They all laugh, except Lynda

(*To Lynda*) Don't worry, love. It gets easier as we go along. (*Swinging round on Doreen and Sandra*) It's not like Enid to sit down. There must be a reason. It wasn't that bloke from Sunday School?

Doreen Sunday School?

Avril The neat one. You must have seen him. The celibate with gloves on.

Doreen Oh—yes—him—yes—him . . .

Avril Was he dancing with her, talking with her, touching her, or anything like that?

Sandra What—an RC with gloves on?
Doreen Er—he was reading to her—
Sandra —with gloves on—
Doreen —from the Bible. He had one with him.
Sandra That's right—he had a condensed version—in his top
pocket—instead of a handkerchief.
Doreen Instead of pencils.
Avril I hardly expected it to be set upon a lectern.
Doreen Maybe she did, that's why she's waiting.
Avril She'll wait for ever.
Sandra Not if she knows how to cope.
Avril (*sarcastically*) Like you, out there.
Sandra Yes. Just now, you'd have been in tucks, doubled up. It
creased me. I had a dance with this fellow—in a nylon shirt
and string vest . . .
Doreen A sort of gorilla in a hair net.
Sandra I danced with him—it wasn't easy, without an anaes-
thetic. We was a beat behind the music, when he asked me—if
I had any erogenous zones. He did, he asked me—in a real
husky voice. "Have you any erogenous zones?" he said. "Oh,
sorry," says I, "but I only carry mints in me 'andbag . . ."

Peals of laughter from everyone except Lynda, who is a bit lost

His face, you should have seen it—it were a picture.
Avril Without a smile?
Sandra He was mad.
Doreen He left?
Sandra Nearly knocked me over in the rush.
Avril (*clicking her fingers at Lynda*) Note that. The power of a
woman's tongue, generally unrecognised. By heck, you're
learning a lot tonight, love. Got it made. What, did I say, gets
easier as we go along. (*To Doreen*) One to mark up, wouldn't
you say, Doreen? One to mark up.

*Doreen takes her lipstick from her handbag and writes a large
figure '1' on the mirror*

Lynda (*pointing across the room*) Oh I say, there's Enid. She's got
her coat on.

*Sandra, Doreen and Avril swing round and gaze in the direction of
Lynda's pointing finger*

Avril Got her coat on? Without a word? Going?

Sandra and Doreen glare angrily at Lynda

Avril (*to Lynda*) Why didn't you say before—sooner . . .
Lynda But I—I only just . . .
Avril You've got to be quick. (*Angrily*) And you two, not tell-
ing me the truth when I asked.

Sandra and Doreen flatten themselves against the wall

Hiding behind religion when I could have done something.
Doreen All the best people do.
Avril What did you say?
Sandra It were the best thing we could do.

*Avril puffs out her cheeks disbelievingly and grabs some article
from the shelf and throws it at Sandra and Doreen missing them*

Don't burst a gasket, girl, it's not worth it. The circumstances,
they were beyond our control.
Doreen She's right. We never thought. We weren't counting on
him coming back. He came back, you see. Came back.
Avril Tell me another. It were a fantasy—all in her mind—
wearing blue—this lark—all in her bloody mind—they never
come back twice, you know that.
Doreen Not never?
Sandra Wrong . . .
Avril Me? Wrong? Wrong about men?
Sandra Keep your hair on—sooner or later we all make mistakes.
Lynda Perhaps Enid's just . . .
Doreen (*to Lynda*) You keep out of this.
Avril You let it happen. It shouldn't have, d'you hear me? It
shouldn't have.
Sandra Shall I tell her, Doreen?
Doreen I wish you would.
Avril ⎫
Lynda ⎭ What? (*Speaking together*)
Avril (*to Lynda*) You keep out of this.
Sandra There's no need to worry, Avril. There's really no need.
Enid's affair won't last.

Doreen and Sandra seat Avril on a stool and kneel either side

Avril Oh . . .
Sandra Yes—well, you see—I've got his wallet. (*She brings out a wallet from her handbag*)

Avril's face breaks into a grin as she takes the wallet in her hand. Sandra brings out more wallets. They all laugh, except Lynda. Doreen then dips into her handbag and brings out a handful of wallets. They are all carefully laid out at Avril's feet

Lynda (*watching*) Oh heck—I never thought it was like this—at a dance.

Doreen and Sandra get up

Sandra Your mother never said?
Lynda You see, I only thought . . .
Doreen Don't.
Sandra Never.
Avril (*to Lynda*) You seem very confused—have one of these. (*She offers a wallet to Lynda, holding it out so that it falls open showing the contents to the audience—money, bank card, photograph, letter and packet of contraceptives. She holds it in this position until the* LIGHTS *fade*)
Doreen As a souvenir.
Avril Go on—touch it. Feel it. It's very personal.

Lynda cannot quite bring herself to do this

Lynda Oh heck, I don't think I want to.
Avril Well, you should, for it's not just hearts and minds you have to get to know—but the influences as well.
Sandra Yes, draw your own conclusions.
Doreen Like us.

The LIGHTS *fade to a—*
BLACK-OUT

FURNITURE AND PROPERTY LIST

SCENE 1

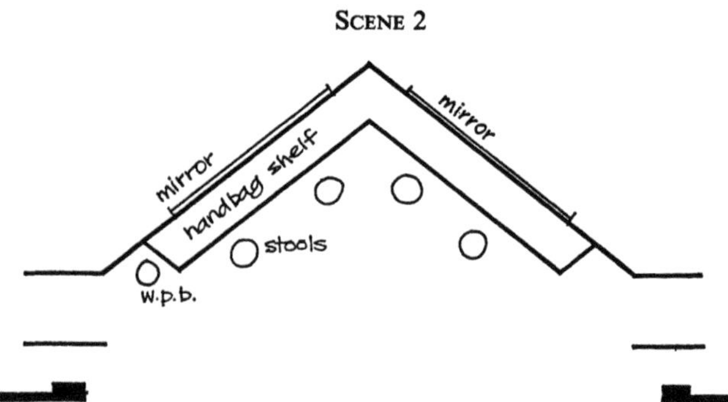

On stage: Street lamp (optional)
Dance-hall poster (optional)

SCENE 2

On stage: Handbag shelves round walls with mirrors above
4 stools (swivel tops if possible)
Wastepaper basket
Ashtray on shelf

SCENE 3

Off stage: Tray with 3 glasses of gin and tonic (**Doreen**)
Glass (**Sandra**)
Several wallets. *In one:* bank notes, bank card, letter photo-
graph, packet of contraceptives (**Sandra** to put in
handbag)
Several wallets (**Doreen** to put in handbag)

Personal: **Avril:** handbag containing tweezers, eyelash curlers, metal
file, nail scissors, large comb, hairspray, eye drops,
dental floss, cigarette packet, lighter; coins

Doreen: handbag containing chewing-gum, small bottle of
Eau-de-Cologne, lipstick, tissues, brush, hairspray; coins

Enid: handbag; coins, blue blouse

Sandra: vanity case containing Max Factor Swedish
formula foundation, gold glitter dust, gold eye shadow,
lipsticks, baby oil, cotton bud, large false eyelashes,
make-up chart, 3 wigs; carrier-bag containing black
dress, pair of shoes, large pair of scissors, box of jewellery

Lynda: handbag; box of chocolates; locket; watch

LIGHTING PLOT

Property fittings required: street lamp (optional), mirror lights
Exterior, a street; interior, a cloakroom

Scene 1.   Night

To open: Street lamp lit (optional) and general effect of exterior street
        lighting

Cue 1   **Avril:** "One and two halves?"   (Page 6)
Fade to Black-out

Scene 2.   Night

To open: Black-out

Cue 2   When set   (Page 6)
Bring up mirror lights and bright interior lighting

Cue 3   **Avril:** "—places, everyone—places"   (Page 18)
Fade to Black-out

Scene 3.   Night

To open: Black-out

Cue 4   When set   (Page 18)
Bring up to previous lighting

Cue 5   **Doreen:** "Like us"   (Page 27)
Fade to Black-out